INCHCOLM ABBEY
AND ISLAND

Description by **Richard Fawcett**
BA, PhD, FSA, FSA(Scot)
History by **David McRoberts**
PhL, STL, D Litt, FSA, FSA(Scot)
with a section on the 20th century defences
by
Fiona Stewart MA, FSA(Scot)

HISTORIC SCOTLAND

EDINBURGH: HMSO

An Island Sanctuary

The foundation of Inchcolm Abbey is said to have been planned by Alexander I after he had been given shelter on the island during a storm by its resident hermit, in 1123. However, the death of the king in the following year prevented the foundation being finalised, and it may not have been until about the 1150s that the new community was formally established as a priory of Augustinian canons.

The first small church was built around that time but, as the priory prospered and grew, it was found necessary to extend it on a number of occasions in the thirteenth century. From that period also dates the earliest of the domestic buildings, the chapter-house. In 1235 the priory's status was increased to that of a full abbey.

During the fourteenth century the abbey's vulnerable position in the Firth of Forth left it prey to devastating attacks by English forces, and it suffered grave damage on a number of occasions; but a period of calm and prosperity followed in the early years of the next century. It was probably during that latter period that both the church and the domestic buildings were almost completely rebuilt.

The corporate religious life of the canons was terminated by the Reformation in 1560, although several continued to live within their old quarters until at least as late as 1578. After the Reformation, parts of the domestic buildings were adapted to serve as a residence for their new owner, and it was because of this – and the abbey's isolated island site – that these buildings survived so completely until they were put to other uses.

The church, however, for which no alternative use was found, was largely demolished.

This guide is divided into three sections. The first provides a short description of what is a fascinating – but can also be a very confusing – group of buildings. The second section gives a brief account of its history. Roads: There are plans at the back. The final section details the island's later history – Inchcolm served as an important coastal defence battery during both World Wars.

2

Church and Cloister

Hog back stone

On the hill beyond the abbey is a memorial of the type usually described as hog-backed, on account of its curved spine, which provides the earliest evidence for the Christian occupation of the island. It is thought to be one of the first of its type in Scotland and probably dates from the mid tenth century. The sloping upper flanks of the stone, covered with tile-like decoration, remind us that such memorials belong to a tradition of shrines and carved stones shaped like houses, and the beasts which grasp each end of the ridge reveal the impact of the art of Scandinavia. Below the 'roof' there are pairs of pilasters on each side, and in addition there is a cross on one side and a figure of a man whose arms may be uplifted in prayer on the other. In the sixteenth century it seems the monument was associated with a standing cross, but no trace now remains of this.

The hermit's cell

To the north-west of the abbey church, in the corner of the garden, there is a small **stone cell**. Traditionally, this is said to have been the hermit's cell in which Alexander I was given shelter in 1123. With its irregular rectangular plan and stone vault it is certainly attractive to think that this cell, with its superficially Irish appearance, was the home of early hermits. But, if it was, it must have been subject to much later rebuilding. In its present form the stone vault can hardly be of a date before the later middle ages, whilst the internally lintelled doorway has an even more recent appearance. It is possible that the door was remodelled after the Reformation, when the cell was used for burial purposes.

4

The hermit's cell.

The first priory church

The priory had rather faltering beginnings and it is unlikely that a church was built for it before the mid twelfth century. This first church was a very simple building of no greater pretensions than most parish churches of its date. It was made up of two rectangular compartments, the eastern of which was probably intended as a chancel, containing little more than the high altar. The nave to its west would have housed the stalls occupied by the canons during the long hours of their services.

Sketch of the church in its likely mid twelfth-century state as viewed from the north.

Only the **nave** of this church survives and much of it has been altered so extensively that it is barely recognisable. The only features which now point to its early date are parts of the processional entrance in the west front, traces of blocked windows and stretches of string courses (horizontal mouldings). The doorway is now covered by a later building, but it has been opened up to reveal the caps and bases of the shafts which would have supported its outer arch; the caps are of the block-like 'cushion' type characteristic of the mid twelfth century. The best evidence for the windows and string courses is to be seen on the south side, within the domestic range above the west side of the cloister, where a blocked round-headed arch can be seen, with a string course above. Traces of windows can also be seen within the upper part of the nave.

After this church was replaced by a new one, built at its east end in the early fifteenth century, a stone **barrel vault** was constructed at a low level within it. This lower level was used for a period as one of the walks around the cloister. The upper level was adapted for occupation, presumably by one of the principal officers of the abbey.

Sketch of the church in its likely earlier thirteenth-century state as viewed from the north.

Additions to the first priory church

The church as first built soon proved inadequate for the expanding community of canons and appears to have been enlarged on more than one occasion, although the precise details of what was done are not always certain. These enlargements took the form of eastward extensions to house the choir of the canons and the presbytery around the high altar more fittingly. But other alterations were made at the same time, such as the insertion of a pair of larger windows in the west wall of the nave, which may now be seen within the building which was later placed in front of it.

On the architectural evidence, soon after about 1200 the original chancel had a handsome **bell tower** raised above it, with a processional door into the cloister on its south side, and an extended eastern limb was added to house the presbytery and choir. The chief interest of the tower lies in the screens which were inserted into its base to separate the canons' choir from the nave,

which had probably come to be at least partly open to lay folk. On the east side was the screen known as the *pulpitum*, which would have had a wall with a central door at its base and which still has the remains of three tall open arches above. On the west side was the rood screen, so-called because of the placing of the great rood or crucifix here. This screen had two doorways to permit the central placing of the main nave altar below the rood, and two tall open arches above it. As originally viewed along the church, the counterpoint between the two sets of arches must have been a very attractive feature. Even in their present mutilated state, they represent a remarkable survival. Particularly worthy of note are the capitals carrying the arches, which have handsome foliage carving of the type known as waterleaf. When the nave had a barrel vault inserted within it, as mentioned earlier, the same happened within the base of the tower, with the consequent destruction of the screen walls below the arches, although evidence of one of the doors through the rood screen can still be seen.

At the upper level of the tower the belfry windows have been considerably altered. Nevertheless, it may be noted that they were originally of two pointed openings within a round arch, with secondary openings cut through the stone at their head. The simple tracery so formed is usually described as plate tracery.

7

An engraving, by Robert Billings, of the interior of the chapter-house in the mid 19th century. (Reproduced by kind permission of the Royal Commission on Ancient Monuments, Scotland.)

The earliest buildings around the cloister

A monastic community required domestic buildings, as well as a church, and the main core of these was usually grouped around a rectangular space known as a **cloister.** Inchcolm has the best preserved cloister in Scotland, although most of what we now see is the result of fifteenth- and sixteenth-century rebuilding and represents a far from typical arrangement. One building is, however, of the early thirteenth century, although its precise place in the development of the cloister is unclear. That building is the **chapter-house**, the meeting place and business room of the community. It is one of only three in Scotland known to have been built as a centralised polygonal structure, the others being at Holyrood (another Augustinian house) and at the cathedral of Elgin. The inspiration for such a plan came from England, where many centralised chapter-houses were built from the twelfth century onwards. A curiosity of this chapter-house is that its handsome entrance doorway faces into the room, rather than out of it as might normally be expected, and that its base is partly covered over. There must thus be at least a suspicion that the door slightly pre-dates the chapter-house and was originally associated with some other structure.

The room is smaller than its counterparts at Holyrood and Elgin and, as a result, no central pier was required to carry its stone vault. Instead, the vault has at its centre a small boss carved with stiff leaf foliage, with a hole at its centre through which a light might be lowered. The focus of the room is a triplet of seats in the east wall for the three principal officers of the community; the other canons would have sat on stone benches around the walls. The chapter-house was originally a single-storeyed structure, but was later heightened by the addition of another room above its vault.

A thirteenth-century mural painting discovered within a tomb recess in the south wall of the church. The upper parts of the figures had been destroyed, but are restored in this view.

Later additions to the abbey church

For the final state of the first church we have little more than a number of tantalising clues. It is recorded that in 1265 Bishop Richard of Dunkeld built a new choir and that the bones of some of his predecessors who had chosen to be buried at Inchcolm were moved into it. Bishop Richard arranged for his own heart to be buried there in 1272 as a sign of his love for the island, although the rest of his body was interred at Dunkeld.

In the course of investigations of the surviving fragments of this extended choir in the 1920s a recess was found on the south side, with the lower part of a painting of a gathering of clerics at its back. It seems likely that this recess belonged to a mural tomb and, since it is known that Bishop Richard had Bishop John de Leycestre (d 1214) re-interred on the south side of the choir, it is assumed that the tomb may have been the latter's. The scene depicted may be intended to portray the entombment of de Leycestre himself.

Another part of the extensions to the church which is likely to have been of the thirteenth century is the addition of a transept (cross arm) on the north side of the tower, the foundations of which were traced by excavation. This transept was in the form of a pair of chapels, to the west of which was a narrower aisle, entered from the nave. Separating aisle and chapels was an arcade of two arches. For reasons which are now uncertain the transept seems to have enjoyed a relatively short life. At a later stage a small projection immediately to its east was added against the choir flank; this was probably a sacristy, where the canons officiating at the altar prepared themselves. After the church itself had been replaced by the new one, yet another transept-like projection was built against the tower, although the prime purpose of this last addition was domestic rather than liturgical. There may also have been a wish to prevent an alarming northward lean of the tower developing further.

Sketch of the church in its likely later thirteenth-century state as viewed from the north.

The second church

The abandonment of the first church, and its replacement by a new one, has already been mentioned several times. The commencement of the rebuilding could have been as early as 1402, when the Lady Chapel (usually identified with the south transept) is said to have been erected by Prior Richard of Aberdour and Canon Thomas Crawford, but it is tempting to link the brunt of the operation with the great historiographer abbot, Walter Bower (1418–49). Certainly we know that building operations were underway during his abbacy, because in 1421 a mason was amongst those saved from drowning in a boating accident. We also know that Bower was architecturally active in other respects, since it was he who first constructed a defensive wall around the abbey precinct, parts of which still remain.

The new church was of cross-shaped plan and must have been a characteristic product of late medieval Scotland. Only part of the south transept stands to any great height, but we can still see that the main space of presbytery and choir ran unbroken from east to west, with arches in the side walls between the two parts which opened into the transepts. The whole was covered by pointed stone barrel vaults. To appreciate how it must have appeared we now have to look to other churches of the later middle ages, such as Dunglass, Crichton or Ladykirk. Unfortunately, some of the vaults must have caused problems, because massive buttresses were added to the north transept to absorb their thrust.

Some of the furnishings provided to enhance the setting of the services have partly survived. In the south wall of the presbytery, next to the entrance to the transept, is a fragment of the *sedilia*, the recessed mural seats on which the priest and his assistants sat at certain points of the service. An even more unusual survival is the *mensa*, the top slab, of the high altar, with its five incised crosses commemorative of the wounds of Christ. This has been re-set on low masonry at the original site of the altar. In the south transept are fragments of one of the two subsidiary altars there. It originally rested on two columns at the outer corners, the bases of which are in fact inverted and re-used capitals, but at a later stage solid masonry was placed between the columns. Also in the transept are two *piscinae*, in which

Sketch of the church in its likely fifteenth-century state as viewed from the north.

the sacred vessels used at the altars were washed, along with an aumbry or wall cupboard. Also inside the transept are preserved considerable extents of the plaster which covered both the walls and – in a thinner application – the carved detail. In the walls on the west side of the transept are traces of timber straps which suggest that there was a wooden lining here at some stage.

The nave of the new church partly overlapped the choir of the old, but a portion of the area occupied by the old choir was left open as a courtyard, and eventually a spiral stair was built in one of its corners to afford access from the rooms which were created at the upper level of the old church. Within the new church a small vestibule was formed at the west end, at the foot of the stairway from the dormitory. However, no nave appears to have been provided for layfolk to worship in; perhaps the island site was felt to make such provision unnecessary by this date.

The construction of the monastic buildings

One of the more perplexing problems of Inchcolm is the date of the main body of monastic buildings around the east, south and west sides of the cloister. That there must have been something on this side of the church by the early thirteenth century is shown by the surviving chapter-house. Yet the provision of a window on the south side of the choir extension, where the dormitory now abuts it, suggests that any buildings associated with the chapter-house must have been lower than those we now see.

The existing buildings, with their barrel vaults at both levels, are probably essentially of the fifteenth century; they are thus unlikely to be far in date from the new church, and must be similarly representative of the abbey's revived fortunes at that time. However, examination of the walls shows that there are considerable differences in the masonry of which they are constructed, suggesting that some earlier work may have been incorporated within them. It was presumably because of the existence of this earlier work that the monastic buildings remained at the side of the old church rather than being reconstructed adjacent to the new church.

A view towards the canons' reredorter, or latrine. On the left is the south cloister walk, with the refectory or dining hall at the upper level.

The layout of the monastic buildings

Inchcolm's monastic buildings are at one and the same time both typical, yet uncharacteristic of such complexes. In common with the great majority of monasteries they are grouped around a cloister against the flank of the church. Also in common with most monasteries, the **canons' dormitory** is at first-floor level of the east range, and the *frater* or refectory (eating hall) is in the south range. But Inchcolm is unusual in that the whole of the ground floor of the three ranges was occupied by covered walks around the cloister, whereas it was more usual for the walks to be in the form of lean-to corridors against the buildings which enclosed the central space. An arrangement like Inchcolm's was sometimes found in English houses of friars, which were usually in urban areas where land was scarce, but it was most unusual elsewhere. However, in Scotland there are two other Augustinian houses – Inchmahome and Jedburgh – where one or more of the walks is absorbed in the adjacent ranges, although in these cases they do not occupy the whole of the range.

We are thus reminded that the Augustinians could be more eccentric in their monastic planning than the other orders. But, even more unusual at Inchcolm, is the way in which the original church was made into one of the cloister walks, and it was presumably for this reason that the stone vault already referred to was inserted. Such a conversion – which now seems almost sacrilegious – has few parallels elsewhere.

The original means of access to all of the principal rooms on the upper floors aroundthe cloister is partly uncertain. The dormitory had two staircases, one for night-time use – which still survives – leading into the church vestibule, and one for day-time use leading into the small courtyard at the west end of the church and from there into the cloister. The **west range,** which probably served as a guest hall for visitors to the abbey, had an external staircase from the courtyard at the west end of the abbey. However, the original means of access to the refectory is unknown. There are now two **stairs**: a straight flight from the west cloister walk and a circular stair from outside the south range. Both of these appear to be of the sixteenth century and the latter partly blocks an earlier window.

In constructing these buildings the memory of the fourteenth-century attacks was evidently still raw, since they were made

Interior of the canons' refectory or dining hall, above the south cloister walk.

as fireproof as possible through the construction of stone barrel vaults at both levels. The most extraordinary of the vaults in the abbey was that constructed in a room formed above the early thirteenth-century chapter-house and reached by a stair from the dormitory. There can be few more ungainly attempts to cover a space anywhere in Scotland. The large fire-place in this room suggests it was intended as a **warming house**, where the canons were allowed to keep the winter cold of the island at bay, although this is certainly a rather unusual position for such a room. Close to the fireplace are traces of moralising texts, perhaps to help the canons to concentrate their minds on higher things.

Although little now survives within these buildings from the time of their occupation by the canons, there are still a few fascinating pointers to the pattern of their life. In the cloister, at the south-east angle, may be seen a **cresset basin**, within which a light would have floated on oil. Further along the south walk is the damaged **lavatory basin** at which the canons washed their hands before ascending to the refectory: above it is a water inlet and below it a drain. The most complete evidence for an aspect of the canons' life is in the **refectory** itself. The **mural pulpit** from which suitable readings were made during meals is in the south wall, and the prominence of the high table is still detectable from the ghost of a curved canopy at the east end. At the opposite end is the fireplace of the small **kitchen** which was formed here at a late period, and which would have been enclosed by a wall or screen. It can be seen that when it was installed a hatch between the refectory and the guest hall had to be blocked. Reminders of a later period, when the monastic buildings were converted to form a house after the Reformation, can be seen in the traces of holes in the walls to take the joists of an inserted ceiling and the fixings for a lath and plaster lining.

The abbey from the north-west. The western range of the cloister lies to the right of the church tower.

Later modifications and additions to the monastic buildings

Reference has already been made to some of the later changes to which the monastic buildings were subjected, such as the insertion of a kitchen and the addition of stairs to the refectory. Another significant change was the construction of a **lean-to walk** of the more conventional type along the north side of the cloister. This presumably indicates that the lower part of the old church was by then required for other uses, although there is nothing to indicate what these uses were. Similarly, we cannot know the precise use to which the upper parts of the church and tower were being put, other than that the large fireplaces inserted in the west wall of the nave and in the tower point to important domestic occupation. By the later middle ages the

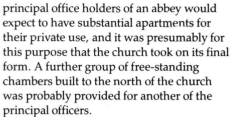

principal office holders of an abbey would expect to have substantial apartments for their private use, and it was presumably for this purpose that the church took on its final form. A further group of free-standing chambers built to the north of the church was probably provided for another of the principal officers.

Another intriguing range of chambers was built to the south-east of the main complex, in a situation which set it apart from the other buildings and also commanded splendid views over the Forth. It has been suggested by some writers that this range was the infirmary, where the old and sick canons might lead a less strict form of life, but its planning does not readily accord with such use and it is perhaps more likely that it was the residence of the head of the community, the abbot. In this position it could share the use of the reredorter (latrine block) at the end of the canons' dormitory, and there was thus at least a nodding acceptance of the communal co-existence required as part of the monastic ideal, however far it might have been in fact diluted in such details.

The **reredorter** itself was a building which gave the canons some difficulties. Such buildings were usually in the form of an extension of the dormitory, with a line of cubicles ranged above the main drain. At Inchcolm the sea took away the waste and the reredorter was a small block on the edge of the island, reached across a bridge from the south end of the dormitory. Unfortunately for the canons, the beach rose progressively in the later middle ages, so that the sea no longer reached the arched openings below the seats. Consequently, a new latrine block had to be built beyond the earlier one and the dormitory was extended to meet it above an arched entrance to the abbey's inner precinct. Parts of this dormitory extension, which is now roofless, show particularly clear evidence of its later adaptation for residential use.

A King's Thanks

The hermits of Inchcolm

Turgot, prior of Durham, writing his life of St Margaret at the beginning of the twelfth century, speaks of the great number of hermits who lived saintly lives in isolated cells throughout Scotland. The site of one of these hermitages appears to have been the island of Inchcolm, or Emonia, in the Firth of Forth. The hermits, who successively inhabited the island, were guardians of a holy place whose reputation for sanctity went back several centuries to the shadowy figure of St Colm, the patronymic saint of the islet. Nothing is known for certain about St Colm but, during the medieval period, he was identified with St Columba, the sixth-century abbot of Iona.

The early sanctity of Inchcolm is attested by the tradition, repeated by Hector Boece, that the Danes, defeated by Macbeth in the battle of Kinghorn, paid a large sum of gold to have their dead interred on the holy isle. In fact, the tenth-century hog-backed tombstone, which still exists on the island, was regarded by Boece as the monument of the Danish leader.

The foundation of the priory

The primitive cell, standing to the west of the ruined medieval monastery (though apparently much restored in the fourteenth and fifteenth centuries) is possibly the actual cell occupied by the hermits of Inchcolm. This hermitage came into prominence in 1123, when King Alexander I and some of his courtiers, crossing the Firth of Forth on business of state, were blown off their course by a south-west gale and, for three days, had

to remain stormbound on the island, where the hermit sheltered them and shared his scanty food with them. A contemporary poem speaks of King Alexander's devotion to St Columba and, stormbound on Inchcolm, the king seems to have identified the tutelar saint of the island with St Columba and, in thanksgiving for his deliverance from the storm, he vowed to build a monastery on the island in the saint's honour.

The kings of the Canmore dynasty, in their work of modernising the Scottish church, introduced a variety of new and progressive religious orders which, at that period, were enjoying popularity in France and England. The religious order for which King Alexander showed marked preference was that of the canons who followed a quasi-monastic rule, vaguely attributed to St Augustine of Hippo, who were known as Canons Regular of St Augustine, Austin Canons, or, from the colour of their religious habit, Black Canons. Of the four Augustinian foundations pro-jected by King Alexander I, only one, the monastery of Scone, was completed: the work of establishing the other three – Inchcolm, Loch Tay and St Andrews – was interrupted by the king's death on 23 April 1124.

Building the priory

The foundation charter of the monastery of Inchcolm has not survived but medieval chroniclers assign it to about the year 1124. However, the beginnings of the monastery are obscure, presumably because the work was upset by the royal founder's death. The exact year when the first Augustinian canons settled on the island is unknown, nor do we know from what older monastery they came. The new king, David I, entrusted Bishop Gregory of Dunkeld (about 1147–69) with the task of administering the endowment of the new priory and of supervising the settlement of the Augustinian community on the island. In the earliest extant charter of the monastery, dating from about 1162–9, Bishop Gregory transfers the property to the canons who are now settled in their new home. The names of two early priors of Inchcolm (probably the first and second), Brice (about 1162–9) and Roger (about 1163–78), appear among the witnesses listed in some contemporary charters.

The circumstances attending the establishment of the priory made it expedient for the new community to seek from the pope a bull confirming its foundation together with its possessions and endowments. This bull, granted by Pope Alexander III in 1178, is addressed to Walter, prior of Inchcolm, and it enumerates the possessions of the priory which consisted of appropriated parish churches and lands together with other income in money and in kind.

Walter was prior of Inchcolm until the year 1210 and it is to his term of office that we should ascribe the large new choir which was added to the east end of the old chancel, and the bell tower which was raised above the earlier choir. Relations between the monastery and the bishops of Dunkeld, in whose diocese the monastery lay, continued to be harmonious. Successive bishops of Dunkeld were benefactors of the priory and, since the place was regarded as a shrine of St Columba, the patron saint of the diocese,

the bishops sought sepulture within its walls. Bishop Richard de Prebenda was buried here in 1210 as also was his successor, Bishop John de Leycestre, in 1214. The monastery attracted many other benefactors, great feudal landowners like the de Quincys, Avenels and Mortimers, as well as humbler folk such as Pagan, a twelfth-century goldsmith of Edinburgh.

Priors and abbots
By the early thirteenth century, Inchcolm priory was fully integrated into the family of Scottish Augustinian monasteries and it played its part in the life of the nation. Prior

The interior of the chapter-house, looking back towards the entrance doorway from the cloister.

Walter, for example, was one of the Scots envoys to Rome in 1182 and, in 1199, he was away on an embassy to England. His name occurs as witness in many transactions of the period and, in 1210, he was appointed abbot of Holyrood. Michael, a canon of Scone, was elected prior at Inchcolm but, within a year, he had died and was succeeded by Simon, who had been sub-prior of Inchcolm. Simon's successor, William, a former canon of Holyrood, proved an unsuccessful ruler and the community had him deposed. Prior Nigel, a former canon and cellarer of Jedburgh, who took his place, was a man of different stamp, wise, devout and good-humoured. The next prior, Henry, was appointed in 1228 and, when Bishop Gilbert of Dunkeld secured from Pope Gregory IX the erection of the priory of Inchcolm into an abbey (May 1235), Henry became the first abbot. Within a few months of this event, Bishop Gilbert died and was buried in the abbey church of Inchcolm.

Worship

There are indications among the surviving charters of the abbey that there was some increase in the solemnity of the liturgical ceremonial of the abbey church at this time. Some time before the year 1249, Bishop Geoffrey of Dunkeld, a zealous promoter of liturgical decorum, made a donation of 20 shillings, from the church of Cramond, for the incensation of the Host at the elevation in the conventual high mass – an early example of a custom which had only recently made its appearance in the cathedral of Paris. A further grant of 20 shillings from the church of Cramond was donated in 1256 by the next bishop of Dunkeld – Richard of Inverkeithing – for the provision of 20 candles to burn at the high altar of the abbey church each year on the vigil and feast-day of St Columba.

This expansion of the liturgical life of the community is reflected in the architectural history of the abbey. In 1265, at the expense of Richard of Inverkeithing, the whole chancel was extended, making it double its former size and, in the following year, the

three bishops of Dunkeld, who had been buried in the abbey church, were re-interred in the new chancel, Bishop Richard de Prebenda and Bishop Gilbert on the north side, near the high altar, and Bishop John de Leycestre on the south side.

Wars and destruction

The end of the thirteenth century was the end of an era for Scotland. The wars of independence exhausted the resources of the kingdom and at Inchcolm, as elsewhere, building operations were suspended and later resumed on a more restricted scale. Brice, abbot of Inchcolm, and Adam, the prior, swore fealty to Edward I, at Berwick, on 28 August 1296. They could not have foreseen that the close friendly relations between Scotland and England were now at an end and that in the three centuries of intermittent warfare which had now begun their own monastery would gradually be brought to complete ruin.

One result of the ravages of the long Anglo-Scottish war is the serious loss of documents illustrating the history of the abbey. In fact, we cannot even recover the names of the abbots who presided over Inchcolm throughout the entire course of the fourteenth century. We have only occasional glimpses of the abbey's life during that century. The first descent of an English ship was in 1315, when an English force landed near the abbey territory at Donibristle and was repulsed by the gallantry of Bishop Sinclair of Dunkeld. Another attack is recorded in the year 1335, when an English ship plundered the monastery, stealing even the statue of the patron saint. The chronicler tells us that the invaders, frightened by a sudden storm at sea, sent the plunder back but, in another visit the following year, they stole the fine carved stalls from the church of Dollar, which was one of the abbey's churches. Each summer brought renewed fear of such raids and it is little wonder that, in one of the choir books written in the abbey at this time, the supplication has been

18

added to a sequence in honour of St Columba, the abbey's patron: 'from all hostile English raids, save this choir which sings thy praise'. This choir book (only a few pages of it survive unfortunately) was written about the year 1340 and testifies to the fact that the canons' life of liturgical prayer continued despite the danger.

There were other disasters in this century. The Black Death visited the land in 1349: we are not told how Inchcolm fared in this calamity but in the sister monastery of St Andrews, 24 of the canons died and that alone would sadly deplete the ranks of the Scottish Augustinian canons. In the English raids, the abbey's charters were stolen or destroyed and this must have proved trouble-some whenever the monastery had to defend its property and privileges. A charter of about 1370, by which Sir William More, lord of Abercorn, renews and confirms the right of the monastery to lands and privileges in the barony of Abercorn, mentions that this is being done because the abbot and community have explained that their original charters and muniments have been stolen and destroyed in wars and other misfortunes. Several charters of like nature illustrate the efforts of the abbey to restore its affairs to a proper footing.

The English returned in 1385. The *Scotichronicon* gives a vivid account of the incident. A great barge from the English war fleet, carrying 140 armed men, came ashore: the raiders plundered the ornaments of the church and the furnishings of the monastery then set fire to an outhouse, whose thatched lean-to roof carried the flames up to the wooden roof of the church. A great crowd of people watched from the shore, expecting the destruction of the whole church, but the wind suddenly veered, the church was saved and the flames were blown back on the soldiers. The soldiers then made off towards South Queensferry, where they encountered some Scots knights and were routed. The damage done to the church at this time may have occasioned the later reconstruction.

The fifteenth century

The more settled political conditions of the fifteenth century brought back stability and prosperity to the abbey. In 1394, John Dersy, abbot of Inchcolm, died: he had been a canon of Cambuskenneth, but we do not know how long he had held the abbacy of Inchcolm. The next superior was Abbot Lawrence, whose name appears in charters from 1399 until his resignation in 1417. In 1402, during his term of office, the vaulted Lady Chapel – which formed the south transept of the church – was erected through the efforts of the prior, Richard of Aberdour, and of one of the canons, Thomas Crawford.

The next abbot received the abbatial blessing from Bishop Robert de Cardeny at Dunkeld on 17 April 1418. He was Walter Bower, a canon of St Andrews, and he was to become the best known of the abbots of Inchcolm. He had scholarship and energy and was the ideal man to restore the fortunes and prestige of the island monastery. His great claim to the gratitude of posterity is the *Scotichronicon*, a history of Scotland from the reign of Malcolm Canmore. This history, written it is said at the suggestion of Sir David Stewart of Rosyth, incorporates the earlier chronicle of John Fordun and continues it down to the death of James I in 1437. The *Scotichronicon* was begun in the year 1441 and, written from an unashamedly patriotic viewpoint, it has preserved for us much information that would otherwise have perished. Where it deals with con-temporary events, it provides a lively picture of the life and outlook of fifteenth-century Scots and the fact that it was widely copied shows that it was an influential book in late medieval Scotland. One of the interesting features of Bower's *Scotichronicon* is the author's gossipy interest in the other Scottish houses of Augustinian canons – Holyrood, Scone, Cambuskenneth and especially St Andrews – showing how the community of Inchcolm regarded themselves not just as canons of one monastery but as members of the wider Augustinian family in Scotland.

Piratical raids by English ships were still a problem and, by an exchange of land with the bishop of Dunkeld in 1408, the canons acquired the mainland property of Donibristle, opposite their island – here the community would live during the summer months when pirate raids were most feared. The structure called 'The Monk's Cave', standing on the shore between Barnhill and Braefoot bays, is probably the remains of the ferry-house and warehouse used by the canons in connection with this property. To obviate this annual disruption of community life, Abbot Bower, some time between 1421 and 1441, fortified the monastery so that the canons could remain on the island even during the dangerous months of summer and autumn.

One of the miracle-stories related by Abbot Bower gives us a fleeting glimpse of the fifteenth-century community: 'It happened moreover in the year 1421 that the abbot of St Columba of Emonia with his community were on the mainland during the summer and autumn, because they did not dare to remain on the island at these seasons for fear of the English. In those days, of course, there did not exist the fortifications by which the monastery is protected nowadays. Accordingly, when the stormy winter weather was at hand and the corn gathered into the barn and the fear of English raids less menacing, the abbot and the brethren, together with the servants and all their gear, went into residence on the island. It was the 25th of October. On the following day, which was a Sunday, the abbot sent the cellarer with some servants to bring over some barrels of beer, which had been brewed at Barnhill, together with other provisions and necessaries. The servant-boatmen, somewhat over-eager and exhilarated, saw not the slightest sign of danger as they moved out from the jetty about three o'clock in the afternoon, with swift oars cleaving the tranquil waters. Then, not content with such progress, they wanted to hoist the sail. Despite the protests of the canons, they had their way and the sail was raised.' The boat floundered in a

sudden squall and 'of the six people who were in the boat, three, namely Alexander the cellarer and two servant-boatmen, were drowned. The other three, namely Dene Peter, a canon, William Bullok, a chaplain, and a stone-mason, were saved in a manner that was not so much astonishing as truly miraculous and so, for the time being, did they evade death.'

The presence of the stone-mason in the unlucky boat is a reminder of the building operations, which seem to have been in progress throughout this time, and Abbot Bower's first-hand experiences of the problems raised by the English raiders must have helped to reinforce the arguments for the Auld Alliance and against any peace negotiations with England which he voiced in the Council General held in the Blackfriars' kirk at Perth in October 1433.

It was probably as a result of the new security, accruing from Abbot Bower's fortification of his monastery, that the place was now occasionally used by the crown as a prison for notable people. The countess of Ross, mother of Alexander, the rebel lord of the Isles, was lodged here during 1431 and 1432; later, in 1478, the unfortunate Patrick Graham, first archbishop of St Andrews, was imprisoned for a time in the abbey.

Richard Augustine Hay asserts that, when Abbot Walter Bower died in 1449 after 32 years in office, he was buried near the high altar of the abbey church. His successor, Abbot John Kers, resigned in 1460 in favour of Abbot Michael Harwar. Of Abbot Harwar we know that he escaped from the shipwrecked 'barge' of the bishop of St Andrews at Bamburgh on 12 March 1472, only to be taken prisoner 'be ane James Kar in Ingland'. Presumably the monastery had to pay the £80 demanded for his ransom.

Vicars and parishes
Augustinian canons frequently acted as vicars in their own dependent parish churches. In 1474 the vicar of Aberdour was John Scott, a canon of Inchcolm, and he

conceived the plan of setting up a hospital in the town. He prevailed on James, first earl of Morton, to endow a hospital in Aberdour, dedicated to St Martha, which would provide shelter and solace to pilgrims and to the poor. It was stipulated that the vicar of Aberdour and his successors in office were to act as rectors of the new foundation. In June 1474, Abbot Michael and the canons of Inchcolm duly accepted responsibility for the management of the hospital. Twelve years later, in 1486, the care of the poor who found shelter in the hospital was entrusted to four nuns of the Franciscan order. The papal mandate of 23 June 1487, confirming this new arrangement, gives credit for the whole enterprise to the vicar, John Scott, stating that all this was done by 'John Scott, a canon of the above monastery (Inchcolm), rector or master and founder of the poor-hospital of St Mary the Virgin (*sic*) near the town of Aberdour in the said diocese (of Dunkeld), considering the spiritual benefits which would arise to the women of Scotland if the Sisters of the said Order were introduced into the Realm'.

Politics

The next two abbots, Alexander Scrimgeour (1490–1) and Robert de Fontibus (1491–2) both resigned after only a few months in office and, in 1492, Abbot Thomas Inglis was appointed. The reason for these resignations is not known, but one suspects royal intervention to make way for a candidate who was able to exert influence at court. Clearly the new abbot was still in his youth, since a royal licence was granted to him, under the Privy Seal in 1498, 'to pas oure the sey to the skulis for science and knaulage to be had, or to the court of Rome in pilgrimage'. His good standing at the court is attested by the charter of 1501, whereby King James IV, 'on account of his special devotion to the blessed confessor, St Columba, and because of the goodwill he feels towards the venerable father in Christ, Thomas, abbot of the monastery of our island of St Columba, and our petitioners, the convent of the same', erected the abbey town of Aberdour-Wester into a burgh of barony. Benevolence was not one-sided for one of the gifts made to King James IV is listed in the 1505 inventory of the

A view into the canons' cloister, looking towards the east range. At the lower level are the arched openings of the cloister walk, with the dormitory windows above.

Chapel Royal at Stirling as 'a large and new Gradual, written by pen on parchment, given to the lord King by the late abbot of Inchcolm'. Abbot Thomas Inglis had died earlier in that year and his successor, Abbot John Elliot, a canon of Holyrood, was provided by the pope to the vacant abbey in June 1505.

John Elliot

The political, social and intellectual unrest, which marked the sixteenth century, could not but affect an institution like Inchcolm Abbey and that larger organisation, the Augustinian order, to which it belonged. However, while James IV was on the throne, peace and prosperity were maintained. In the halcyon days before Flodden, King James IV, on several occasions, visited the island monastery. In 1508, for example, Inchcolm was included in a royal progress, which took in several places around the Firth. On 30 June, James IV was shooting seafowl at the Isle of May, then by way of Pittenweem, St Monance, Kinghorn and Aberdour, he came to Inchcolm on 1 July and spent the night there, leaving the next day by boat for Leith. The music-loving king would have been present at the conventual high mass and one wonders if, on the occasion, the canons sang one of the masses composed by their abbot, John Elliot, who was a notable composer. Writing in 1530, Robert Richardson, an Augustinian canon of Cambuskenneth, who was highly critical of the musicians of his own order in Scotland, denounced the florid compositions of some canons (no doubt referring to such ornate masses as those composed by Robert Carver, canon of Scone about 1503–46), but is full of praise for Gregorian chant and simple compositions 'such as are the masses composed by that devout and religious man, the abbot of St Columba, the outstanding exemplar of our whole Order in Scotland'.

In this final period of tranquillity the number of canons in the monastery was at least 15, as we can see from charter-signatures. One or two books survive from the abbey's early sixteenth-century library, which show the canons to have been men of varied intellectual interests. The daily routine of mass and divine office followed the immemorial traditions of the place and occasional records survive to show the relations of the house with the national life. In November 1532, for example, with the renewal of hostilities against England, the monastery was used as a detention place for an English canon. The Lord High Treasurer noted in his accounts: 'Item, to Johne Stewart and Johne Trinsche, to pas with ane boit to Sanct Columbis inche with the Inglis channoun to be kepid thair . . . xiiijs'. The following January, the unwelcome summons was received by various abbeys, including 'Sanct Columbis Inche, to send thair houshaldis to the bordour'. There were also local problems, as when the abbot and community were summoned, in 1533, to appear in an action, raised against them by George Henderson of Fordell, concerning a coal-pit in the abbey's lands of Bucklyvie which, it was alleged, had been worked within Henderson's lands of Fordell.

Abbot John Elliot was succeeded in 1532 by Abbot Richard Abercromby. It was a sign of the growing decadence of the times that a certain Roman curial official, Bartolomeo Ferrari, tried to secure the appointment, so as to have the emoluments of the office, while remaining an absentee abbot. King James V assured the pope, Clement VII, that the canons of Inchcolm led a most exemplary life, asked him not to appoint anyone who was not of the Augustinian order and insisted that Richard Abercromby, canon of Cambuskenneth, should be appointed.

The commendators

The ineffectual government of Scotland during the minorities of James V and of his daughter, Mary Queen of Scots, together with the crippling English invasions, left the country quite incapable of stemming the tide of change which flowed in from Europe. In the financial chaos, noblemen cast envious eyes on the property with which their

The octagonal chapter-house, with the warming house above. Beyond it is the end of the canons' dormitory.

ancestors had endowed the church. The new theological opinions from Europe and the example of Henry VIII's takeover of monastic property in England seemed to provide warrant for a similar action in Scotland.

The process started at Inchcolm in 1543, when Abbot Abercromby was induced to resign in favour of James Stewart, the thirteen-year-old son of Sir James Stewart of Beath. Thus that family gained control of the temporalities of the monastery, though Abbot Abercromby continued until his death on 26 March 1549 to preside over the religious life of the community. There were notable events during Abercromby's tenure of office. Thomas Forret, one of the canons and vicar of the church of Dollar, was accused of Lutheranism and put to death at Edinburgh in 1539. In an attack by the English, in 1542,

the church was pillaged and some buildings were burnt. Again, after the battle of Pinkie, an English garrison occupied the island from September 1547 until March 1548, the community being given asylum in the Augustinian monasteries of St Andrews, Scone and Cambuskenneth, and in the Benedictine monasteries of Dunfermline, Arbroath, Paisley and Lindores. In August 1548 the canons were back and the place was 'kept by Frenshe men'.

The commendatory abbot, James Stewart, was not present at the Provincial Council, held in Edinburgh in November 1549, which stipulated, as part of its plan to restore the position of the church, that Inchcolm should send two canons for university education and should set aside the vicarage of Leslie as a benefice to maintain a preacher. We do not

know if the commendator implemented these decisions. By 1559, the abbey tenants of Donibristle, Barnhill and Grange were complaining about 'rack-renting'. In the following year, James Stewart joined the Lords of the Congregation and he is numbered by John Knox among those present at the Reformation Parliament, held in August 1560.

We can be certain that the centuries-old routine of solemn mass and divine office came to an end in 1560 in the church. No new canons were admitted, but the community still had a legal existence as a property-owning corporation and the signatures of those canons who survived were necessary for all transactions concerning the property of the abbey. The surviving canons were legally entitled to a pension and

A photograph of the abbey from the south-west in about 1880. The monastic buildings are still in use as a residence, with an entrance at the base of the external refectory staircase. (Reproduced by kind permission of the Royal Commission on Ancient Monuments, Scotland.)

to their 'chamber' and 'yard' in the monastery precincts. The last document, which bears the signatures of canons of Inchcolm, is a charter of 1578, which was signed at Inchcolm by 'Dominus Johne Brounhill' and 'Dominus Andro Anguss'. With these two representatives the community, or 'convent', of Inchcolm disappears from history.

In 1581, James Stewart, the commendator, was created Lord Doune and he had his son, Henry Stewart, appointed commendator of Inchcolm in his place. Thirty years later, the abbey lands of Inchcolm were erected into a secular lordship and Henry Stewart was confirmed in their possession by an Act of Parliament of 1611, which gave him the title of Lord St Colme. He was succeeded by his son, James, on whose death the title passed to the earl of Moray.

Part of the domestic buildings now became the commendator's mansion and in 1581 the abbey church was at least partially demolished by the commendator for, in that year, the ashlar and 'thack stanes' were sold to the Town Council of Edinburgh for the rebuilding of their Tolbooth. In that year also, 'Ille witht the abbay, mansioun, dowcat and yairdis' were feued by Lord Doune to the earl of Moray and the Act of Parliament, ratifying this infeftment, speaks of the place as 'left desert and the same hes bene receptakle to Piratis'.

The island served as a quarantine station for plague-stricken ships entering the Firth of Forth in the late sixteenth and early seventeenth centuries. In the 1790s a Russian hospital was accommodated here to serve the Russian fleet, lying in the Forth and, during the Napoleonic War and First and Second World Wars, fortifications were erected on the island. Apart from these happenings, the post-Reformation story of the island has been uneventful. Finally in 1924, the earl of Moray placed the ruins in state care. Since that time, the ruins have been cleared of later accretions and now form one of the most interesting and picturesque medieval monastic ruins in Scotland.

War Time Garrison

Inchcolm and the defence of the Forth

The history of Inchcolm does not end with the demise of the Augustinian Abbey but continues through to the twentieth century. By this time the island was seen as an important element in the defence of the Firth of Forth, garrisoned by the Army and heavily armed. Visitors may walk around the island and view the surviving military remains but must take care, particularly near cliff edges.

With the outbreak of the First World War in 1914 the Firth of Forth became one of the most heavily defended estuaries in the United Kingdom. The naval base at Rosyth was nearing completion; there was an anchorage for the fleet to the west of the Forth Railway Bridge, itself a vital communication line between south and north; and Scotland's capital city, Edinburgh, lay on the southern shore of the Firth. All these were targets for an enemy, particularly as the Forth's northerly position made it highly vulnerable to attack from German warships – this threat was reinforced in December 1914 when the Germans bombarded Scarborough and Hartlepool on the east coast of England. To counter this potential danger a defensive scheme was devised, implemented and later amended as defensive considerations altered during the progress of the War. The main feature of the scheme was the provision of three defence lines across the Forth, requiring the construction of gun batteries on the shores to the west of Edinburgh and on the Fife coast opposite, and complemented by batteries on numerous islands in the Firth. By this means, gunfire from land and offshore-based artillery could sweep the whole channel of the Forth making

it extremely hazardous for enemy ships to attempt to head up river. In 1914, the Outer Line, from which hostile craft would first come under fire, comprised batteries at Kinghorn and Inchkeith. The Middle Line had batteries at Braefoot Point and Downing Point on the north shore and Hound Point on the south shore. The Inner Line, which was intended to deploy weapons against lighter and faster warships, such as motor torpedo boats, which might penetrate the other defences, had batteries at Carlingnose and Coastguard at the north end of the Forth Bridge, and at Inchgarvie and Dalmeny at the south end.

Inchcolm in the First World War

At the outbreak of War only two of the islands in the Forth – Inchkeith and Inchgarvie – were fortified. However, when, in the early stages of hostilities, the naval anchorage was moved to the east of the railway bridge, the defences as a whole moved in an easterly direction forcing the closure of some batteries, including Carlingnose, Braefoot and Dalmeny, and the construction of new ones including those at Leith and Pettycur which were incorporated in the Outer Defence Line. The island of Inchcolm now formed part of the Middle Line which also included the new batteries at Cramond Island and Inchmickery while the Inner Line comprised the batteries at Hound Point, Inchgarvie, Coastguard and Downing Point.

In addition, the approaches to the anchorage were defended by booms and heavy anti-submarine nets. Not surprisingly Inchcolm now received its complement of guns and searchlights. It was to be a heavily fortified island with eight quick-firing 12 pounder (Naval) guns, subsequently increased to two 6-inch breech loaders (the shells for which weighed 100 lbs), four 4-inch quick firers, which each had a range of about 13,000m (approximately 8 miles), four 4.7-inch quick firers, the concrete aprons for which can still be seen at the west end of the island, and two of the original complement of eight 12 pounder naval guns. In the event the guns were never needed and when the War ended in 1918 they were retained on a 'care and maintenance' basis, ready to be brought back into service in the event of renewed hostilities. One notable event witnessed by the gunners on Inchcolm during the First World War was in 1916 when Vice Admiral Sir David Beatty, Commander of the Battlecruiser Fleet, led his fleet out from Rosyth to take part in the Battle of Jutland. It would be an impressive display of naval strength which the garrison witnessed heading eastwards as the fleet numbered six battlecruisers, four battleships, twelve light cruisers, twenty-nine destroyers and one seaplane carrier all led by Beatty in his flagship 'Lion'.

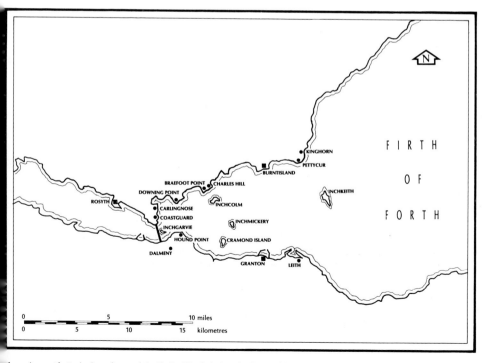

The main coast batteries in and around the Firth of Forth during the First and Second World Wars.

Inchcolm in the Second World War
In 1930 the guns on Inchcolm were either transferred to other batteries, returned to depots or broken up and used as scrap. But nine years later, on the outbreak of the Second World War, the island once again had to be fortified. Searchlights were installed by the Royal Engineers and the Royal Artillery soon took over the manning of the defences, which now comprised two 12-pounders (on the site of the old 6-inch battery) and two 2-pounder 'pom-poms' (machine guns). Until the construction of more permanent buildings was completed temporary accommodation for the garrison was provided in the abbey – the officers slept in the warming house above the chapter house and the other ranks in the rooms above the cloister walk. Transporting the guns to the high ground at

One of the twin 6-pounder guns on Inchcolm during the Second World War. These guns were able to command the area of the Forth north and east of the island by pivoting round on their central circular mounting. (Reproduced by kind permission of The Trustees of the Imperial War Museum, London.)

he east end of the island was a long and firing task. The narrow gauge railway track which ran from the searchlights beside the pier to the batteries above could not be used as it was too steep and in poor condition. In 1940 two twin 6-pounders (one mounted close to the site occupied by the 4-inch guns during the First World War) and a Bofors anti-aircraft gun were added to the fire power, the latter sited at the west end of Inchcolm. Another Bofors was subsequently erected at the east end of Inchcolm to cover the boom which ran between it and the island of Inchmickery to the south east.

One of the two 12-pounder guns on Kent Battery, Inchcolm, so called after a visit to the island by the Duke of Kent in 1939. The large concrete obstacle to the left of the photograph was so placed to prevent the gun swinging round and inadvertently firing on the twin -pounders nearby. The stones in front of the gun acted as camouflage making it less easy for the enemy to identify the site of the battery om the air. (Reproduced by kind permission of The Trustees of the Imperial War Museum, London.)

The garrison on the island during the Second World War numbered about 500 men and included not only the Battery Commanders and gunners but also the District Officer who looked after the equipment, searchlight operators, telephonists and cooks. The guns were manned day and night and the powerful searchlights throughout the hours of darkness, ready to be exposed at a moment's notice to illuminate something suspicious seen or heard at sea. Lookouts maintained a constant watch. During the War the Forth saw relatively little enemy air activity although the first German raid to reach Britain actually took place close to the Forth Bridge on 16 October 1939. Throughout the War the Germans regularly dropped mines in the Forth and, on occasion, also offloaded any bombs which they had not dropped in their raids on targets in the west of Scotland. Although anti-aircraft guns on both sides of the Forth were brought into action on these occasions the bombers were outwith the effective range of these guns.

The Forth was an important waterway and because of the possibility of German mines the Navy regularly had to send minesweepers to keep clear a safe channel which passed south of Inchcolm and north of Inchkeith. The garrison on Inchcolm frequently saw the destroyers of the Rosyth Escort Force setting out on (or returning from) their duties of protecting the east coast convoys. The other channels, which were mined by Britain to deter German attack on the anchorage, were 'no go areas' for all shipping, merchant or naval.

By November 1943, the threat of invasion having receded, the batteries on Inchcolm were put on a 'care and maintenance' basis except for the searchlights which were still required to illuminate the booms protecting the naval anchorage. Although so heavily fortified during the two World Wars, Inchcolm, like so many coast batteries around Britain, was never called upon to fire on an enemy ship. The fact that the guns and gunners were there was a sufficient deterrent.

Inchcolm today

The military installations are now in a ruined state following their deliberate demolition by engineers from the Territorial Army in the early 1960s. At the east end of the island the emplacements for the two 12-pounder and two twin 6-pounder guns can still be seen. So can the observation post and the war shelters, the latter where the soldiers could relax during breaks from duty, generally at night. The shelters were sited close to the guns so that the gun detachments could take part in any necessary action without delay. Visitors can also walk through the brick tunnel constructed during the First World War to provide easy covered access for troops moving from their accommodation on the west side of the island to the batteries on the east. Also surviving are the engine rooms, searchlight emplacements and District Officer's Store, where spare gun parts were kept. On the west side of the island, the officers' mess and quarters, the recreation and parade grounds and barrack blocks are all gone but the First World War 4.7-inch gun emplacements and Battery Commander's Post (used as the Fire Control Post during the Second World War) survive, as does that most invaluable institution, the brick-built NAAFI canteen.

The strictly functional, hurriedly constructed, brick and concrete remains of Inchcolm's twentieth-century war-time rôle stand in stark contrast to the architectural splendour of the medieval Augustinian Abbey. Nevertheless they are an important part of the island's long, rich and varied history.

John of Fordun and Walter Bower (with an introduction by Walter Goodall) *Scotichronicon*, 2 vols, (1759). David MacGibbon and Thomas Ross, *The Ecclesiastical Architecture of Scotland*, vol 2 (1896). J Wilson Paterson, 'The Development of Inchcolm Abbey', *Proceedings of the Society of Antiquaries of Scotland* 60 (1925–6) 227–53. J T Lang, 'Hogback monuments in Scotland', *Proceedings of the Society of Antiquaries of Scotland* 105 (1972–4) 206–35 (Inchcolm on page 227). Richard Fawcett, *Scottish Medieval Churches* (1985).

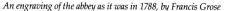

An engraving of the abbey as it was in 1788, by Francis Grose

Plan of the lower level of the abbey

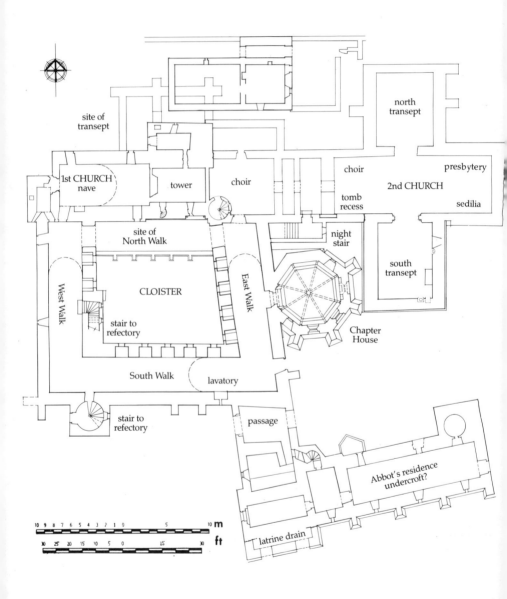

site of
transept

north
transept

1st CHURCH
nave

tower

choir

choir

presbytery

2nd CHURCH

tomb
recess

sedilia

site of
North Walk

night
stair

south
transept

West Walk

East Walk

CLOISTER

stair to
refectory

Chapter
House

South Walk

lavatory

stair to
refectory

passage

Abbot's residence
undercroft?

10 9 8 7 6 5 4 3 2 1 0   5   10 **m**

30 25 20 15 10 5 0   15   30 **ft**

latrine drain